Grasp

finding focus
in a blurry world

Copyright 2016
Michael M. Middleton

> "Our hearts are restless
> until they rest in Thee..."
> *Saint Augustine, 354-430 AD*

All Scriptures NKJV
copyright 1984 by
Thomas Nelson Publishers
Used by permission.

Lamentation

We had life…
life simple and complete,
filled with joy and peace
in their fullest measure.
No asphalt…
but stone
and living waters
and flowered meadows.
No smog…
but silver mists
and glassy seas
and unyielding tranquility.

But we chose a lie, thinking God selfish.

And so all of our brittle days
we wander this maddening maze
grasping for Eden.

Introduction

Take a walk with me... That's right, grab your shoes and get a move-on! We've got places to go and things to do. If you happen to have already retired for the day, that's ok. No need to throw a raincoat on over those pajamas; this is a walk down memory lane.

Take a moment and picture in your mind the last time you were in the bustling heart of a big city. Perhaps you have spent time in New York, Chicago, Atlanta, or Los Angeles? Have you ever strolled through Grand Central Station or a major international airport such as John F. Kennedy, Chicago O'Hare, or Washington Dulles? Perhaps you've stood on the trading floor of a major stock exchange or have braved the 'running of the bulls' at any major department store on Black Friday morning. Whichever of these scenarios best suits your present fancy, focus on that moment.

Now, what do you see? How would you describe your surroundings? Peaceful, calm, serene...a nice place to do some quiet reading? Or perhaps some other adjectives come to mind... like *frantic, stressful,* or *just plain nuts*? It seems as though everyone is desperately rushing in search of something. Many of them don't really know for what they seek. They just know that something is missing which they feel a desperate longing for. So they grasp for one trinket after another, only to find themselves still empty. Yet on they rush through a mindless sea of excesses, ever in search of the next trinket--- be that a big-screen television, a trophy wife, or the vice-presidency in charge of new accounts. They have no true joy in life because life for them is just an exhausting, frantic blur. They fritter away their weeks, months, and decades like hamsters on a wheel… running like mad and getting nowhere.

Now, pause for a moment; take your eyes off of the crowd and find a mirror. What do you see there? No, not that gray hair. Ignore for the time being the puffy eyelids, that weird freckle, that scar from when you were learning to ride a bike… Look deeper. Can you see shades of that same frantic blur in your own life?

Unfortunately, the *hamster wheel* is simply the defining reality of our modern world. But, my friend, this is not what the world was meant to be. Life was not meant to be blurry. We were created not for strife, but for relationship--- not for struggle, competition, and frantic pursuit, but for simplicity and joy. We were made for something far higher than trinkets could ever offer.

It is not that we have too little which leaves us feeling empty, but that we have too much. We have crammed too many useless trinkets into our lives which rob us of the focus we were meant to have, a love relationship with our Creator. Individually, we as Christians are meant to be lights, guiding stars for those with whom we rub shoulders on a daily basis. (Philippians 2:15) Collectively, as the body of Christ, we are meant to be *the light of the world*. (Matthew 5:14) But light only has *real* power when it is focused. An acutely focused beam of light can burn through a steel bar, but loses its power quickly when diffused. In like manner, when we lose our proper focus, when our lives begin to blur and blend in to the same frantic pace around us, we poorly serve the Father of Lights.

Amidst the dim and blurry world we are all immersed in as residents of this modern society, we must examine our hearts and our habits, seeking to increase our focus on that which truly matters. Focus brings power and clarity of purpose. We must learn to set aside frantic, fruitless distractions. In doing so, we will find ourselves much closer to the purpose for which we were created.

I was blessed to play for a rather successful high school football team. (Everyone knows that winning in sports is much more fun than losing.) One thing which our coach emphasized with great regularity was focus. Being a nose-guard, my particular focus was generally along the lines of, "Kill the guy with the ball…" Occasionally, however, I would sub in on special teams. In fact, my very first play of high school football was on kickoff-return.

The coach's instructions were very simple: "Pick a guy and hit him…" Running down the field, I chose my man. Ignoring the cheering crowd and the rest of the players, I zeroed in. Intent on fulfilling my role on the team, I focused intensely on every shift of his stride, adjusting mine to match, fully committed that he would not pass.

A collision of spectacular proportion ensued and I found myself half-dazed, flying backward, slamming onto my back on the turf. Glancing up, I was exuberant to note that my opponent also lay on his back a number of yards away. We had apparently met with nearly identical force and ricocheted off of one another like a couple of billiards balls. Though we both had been knocked down…hard…I had accomplished my task, preventing him from getting to our ball runner. **He did not pass**. The crowd cheered loudly and I distinctly heard the coach screaming from the sideline, "WOO-HOO! Way to go, *Maynard*…

Search and de-stroy!"

It is the deepest yearning of my heart to one day hear something along these same lines from someone far greater than Coach Kramer. Each of us who call ourselves *believers* yearn to hear our Lord say to us, "Well done, good and faithful servant…" (Matthew 25:21) We all yearn to know that we have pleased our Lord. In order for us to accomplish the purpose for which we were created, we need to foster a fuller understanding of what that purpose is and how we may focus our lives toward that goal.

I hope within these pages to sharpen our understanding of what that original purpose was, how we have gone astray from that purpose, and how we may begin to refocus on the things which truly matter. I hope to expose some of the tactics of the enemy which distract us from this end and to encourage the reader to return to a simpler, more focused way of life. May we all learn to live lives of greater clarity, simplicity, and focus in a frantic and blurry world.

Dreams

I dreamed a dream
of wonderful things
in a land where life was slow…
where fountains of grace,
flowing freely,
refreshed the wandering soul.
A gentle path
through valleys bright
along the healing stream
turned back the years
to simpler times,
when dreamers dared to dream.

Chapter One
The Glory Which Was

Two physicists and a theologian walk into a bar… Sounds like the beginning of a corny joke, right? Well, it just so happens to be a humorous sentiment which sprang to mind as I contemplated how to begin this chapter. I have always had a keen interest in two particular areas of study: scientific revelations in Scripture and a deeper Hebraic understanding of Scripture. In pursuing the study of these two fields I am continually amazed at the depth of revelation and innumerable facets of understanding which reveal themselves to the mind which cares to see.

I have benefitted greatly over the years from the study and teaching done by a wide variety of speakers, teachers, and authors. While I am sure that I could compile a much more extensive list of those I have benefitted from in these specific areas, three individuals in particular come to mind. The two physicists happen to be Dr. Carl Baugh, founder of the Creation Evidences Museum of Glen Rose, Texas and Dr. Gerald Schroeder, an Israeli physicist and author. Dr. Schroeder made numerous appearances alongside the late Zola Levitt, founder of Zola Levitt Ministries and co-producer (along with Jeffrey Seif) of the Institute of Jewish Christian Studies, which I completed a number of years ago. Zola, of course, is the theologian in question. I am not sure these individuals would ever be found hanging out in a bar together, but I could definitely picture them in lively discussion over coffee and bagels...

Along with personal study, experiences, and the contributions of others such as Keith Green, Winkie Pratney and Chuck Missler, these three men have greatly enriched my understanding of Scripture and of its author. Much of what I reference in allegorical form in this chapter draws heavily upon their contributions. In lieu of compiling an exhaustive bibliography for what is shared herein, I would simply like to advise you to seek out materials by these great teachers and authors for yourself. I believe that your own walk will be greatly enriched by doing so.

***

Have you ever contemplated what life would have been like had Eden never been lost? What would mankind's day to day reality be like if our first parents had not fallen for the enemy's clever scheme? I am firmly convinced that God knows every moment, every eventuality of time and eternity. Thus, I am convinced that He foreknew the unfortunate choice they would make and had already planned a solution to their failure, for the author of Scripture refers to Himself as, "...the Lamb slain *from the foundation of the world.*" (Revelation 13:8)

   Although God foreknew the painful and difficult path the redemption of mankind would actually take, I am convinced that He, nonetheless, held treasured in His mind and heart what the ultimate good could have been, had they chosen rightly. Let us now use what may be discerned from both science and Scripture, as well as a healthy dose of sanctified imagination, to peek behind the veil of what might have been… What is that *something more* which each of us intuitively knows is missing?

***

<u>Beauty Hurts</u>

To smell, but not taste… To hear muffled, as through a wall, faint echoes, dying away to cold silence. To see pale reflections in a broken, dirty glass; to perceive yet not touch what was meant to be when the golden light of Heaven first fell upon the silver mists of a newborn Earth… and molten jewels sang in the evening and morning skies.

Faint remembrances of a glory nearly forgotten tears at the hearts of Adam's sons. Shadows only… an uncertain memory, like a lullaby your mother once sang. Paradise lost, now lying somewhere distant beyond the horizon. An ancient glory now hides somewhere beyond the veil of time. When time shall at last die away, having run its full course, then… oh, then the glory shall live again!

But what agony to be now so in-between; to smell, but not taste… to hear only echoes… to yearn for, but not grasp.

...As dawn nears, your senses are caressed and aroused by a carefully synchronized unfolding of glory. As you feel yourself waking, you inhale deeply and a warm, gentle breeze perfumed by freshly-flowering honeysuckle greets you. Although the sun is still well below the horizon, it is not dark. In fact, it is never truly dark. The firmament, set in the sky by the Creator, acts as a built-in night light, transferring a portion of the sun's radiance from well beyond the horizon as a gentle pink glow throughout the night.

That same firmament magnifies and intensifies the light of the stars, making them to appear in their true colors. Like molten jewels they shine in myriad hues of yellow, orange, blue, green, red… a cosmic display of grandeur above. Ah, yes! And they *sing* as well! The morning stars quite literally sing for joy! (Job 38:7) Their music travels through the vastness of space as radio waves. The firmament (*Hebrew: "Raqiya"; a thin sheet of metal, most likely hydrogen in its crystalline form…*) tunes in these waves and broadcasts them as audible sound. It fills the atmosphere with a symphony at once soothing and invigorating. Pulsars and quasars keep rhythm and the stars and planets sing together like flutes, oboes, and violins in myriad, ever-changing harmonies, all tuned in the key of C.

You again deeply inhale the perfumed air and open your eyes. You lay in the soft grass of an open field, under a fruit tree on a slight rise. The warm, hairy mass under your head and shoulders shifts slightly and you glance back to see the muzzle of an enormous lion inches from your face. No… there is no fear in your heart, not even the slightest trace. Here, the lion eats grass, not people. (Isaiah 11:7) You recognize this gentle beast as 'Jasper'; the funny little trail of spots on his nose is unmistakable. As his huge, soft, hairy head nuzzles into yours, you reach up and scratch behind his ears, just as he likes it.

You are not homeless; you spend many nights out in this serene meadow not because you must, but simply because you enjoy it. (And, so does Jasper…) A short distance away you have a splendid home, hand-crafted and meeting your every need and desire in every way. But this meadow is one of your favorite places and you never need worry about rain or cold or of falling prey to thieves or dangerous animals. These things simply do not---have not ever existed. Also completely unknown are things like locks, lawyers, doctors, taxes, sleeping pills, politicians, and funeral homes; there's no need for any of those things here. Everyone lives by the law of love and on the very rare occasion there is a misunderstanding or disagreement, chooses to prefer peace to proving oneself right.

You give Jasper one final enthusiastic nuzzle and rise to your feet. You grab a little breakfast from the tree you've slept under and get a long, cold drink from the pure, crystal stream nearby. You stretch the muscles of the perfect body you've lived in for several thousand years now. No gray hairs, or wrinkles, or ulcerative colitis here... You live constantly bathed in the very tangible presence of the giver of life Himself. Never having been separated from that presence by a sinful act of self-will, you know nothing of death or decay. "Good morning, Father!" you whisper to the ever-present glory.

Simultaneously in your spirit and with ears of flesh you hear, ***"Good morning. dear child... Won't you come and walk with Me?"***

You spend the next few hours casually strolling and conversing with your Creator. Through meadows and forests and alongside rushing streams you roam, observing the glories of His creation. Plants and animals of every kind and description display the wonders of His wisdom and infinite creativity. Though you have lived thousands of years, each day there are new mysteries and levels of understanding to explore. After all, you are a finite creature, while He is infinite…unbounded in every way. There will never be a time when you run out of things to learn from Him and you cherish every moment you spend with Him on these walks. And He cherishes you.

When the sun has risen high in the sky, you gather with a number of other blessed children of the Creator. There are a few tasks you've decided to accomplish together this day. In another age, or another kind of world, one might refer to this as "work", but here it is a simple joy. There is nothing taxing, stressful, or strenuous in it. It carries a much different purpose here than the unthinkable rationale of *earning one's bread*. Work, here in this world, is simply a means of fellowship, a way to spend time together in a task which benefits all. It is not about earning anything for yourself, but about giving to others and building relationship.

A delightfully vibrant meal is eaten together, followed by childlike games and song. Discussion goes on until very late in the day as each one in turn shares the various jewels of wisdom and understanding they gained from the Great Father that day. Here, people like Einstein and Nicholas Copernicus are on equal footing with others like plain-old Dave Smith or Lisa Edwards. Every individual is endowed with gifts perfectly suited to bless both them and those around them in special, unique ways. There is no prideful ego and no self-loathing shame. Each individual glories in and freely shares the special and particular gifts and revelations granted them and equally cherishes and appreciates those granted to others. There is not the slightest hint of envy anywhere.

As evening comes, a campfire is kindled. Neither the heat nor light is needed, but there is something cheerful in its glow, something which draws friends together around it and silently speaks of wonders none of them yet know how to express in words. As the stars begin to gleam in their full rainbow-brilliance once again, a final joyous hymn is sung in collective adoration to the giver and sustainer of life. Bidding one another good-night, each one strolls off through the meadow, caressed by the stirring of evening breezes. You begin to pace off towards your home, but notice something off in the distance. There, atop the little rise where you began this day, Jasper is waiting for you...

In Heaven's Fields

Wooden swords and bubble gum

and fireflies at night…

blackberries and campfires

and other such delights…

these are the things

that cheer the hearts

of the young and aged too…

and when we play

in Heaven's fields

beyond the veil of blue,

I'd make a bet

that there we'll find

a wooden sword or two.

Chapter Two
Paradise Lost

I would hope that you now hold before the eyes of your heart at least a vague picture of what God's intention for mankind was when He first spoke, "Let there be…" *Surely such a world…such an existence is too wondrous to imagine,* you might think…and such is true. But there is more. Remember, I have only provided a fleeting representative sketchbook image of a reality which was in truth far grander than it is even possible to understand from our current frame of reference.

The good news (you might say, 'Gospel') is that this glory, so currently beyond our comprehension, will one day be restored, for *"Eye has not seen, nor ear heard, nor have entered into the heart of man the things which God has prepared for those who love Him."* (1 Corinthians 2:9) Yes, for all who choose it, a restoration of that original glory lies just beyond the horizon. At the culmination of the ages we shall stroll the fair meadows of Eden once more.

We shall discuss this great restoration later. For now, let us dwell upon the world as we currently know it. Let us begin by examining just how it was that we found ourselves as a race in such a messed-up state of affairs. How is it that we fell from a place of perfect joy, peace, and endless vibrant health to the dismal abode of strife, illness, and death which we now call "reality"? How is it that warfare, cancer, and poverty are now normal and suicide is a leading cause of death in many people groups? Why are so many so desperate to escape day to day reality that they will willingly pump into their veins chemical substances akin to drain cleaner?

Any self-respecting Sunday School graduate will quickly chime in with, "Why, that's easy…because Adam ate that apple!" While it is certainly true that this account of mankind's fall from innocence was the beginning of our current mess, it is not as simple a matter as it may at first appear. You see, there is much more going on here than the one act of eating that forbidden fruit. And, no, the Bible does not specify it as an apple…but I digress. Tasting that toxic little snack, whatever form it took, was simply a symptom, not the illness. It was in many ways not the original sin of mankind, but a result of other sin, and itself led to even more sin.

Now, what do I mean here by *sin?* Ah, yes, it may help you to understand my point if I were to clearly define that particular theological concept... Simply put, sin is anything which separates us from God. God made us for relationship; sin is any barrier to that relationship. We were created to grow in relationship to God and to become more and more like Him in character. Sin is anything unlike God's character.

Read again the **third chapter of Genesis** and let us make a detailed examination of the progression of sin presented therein.

<u>Adding to God's Word:</u> When tempted by the serpent, Eve at first responds appropriately, stating that they were permitted to eat of any tree of the garden but the one in the middle of the garden. However, she then made her first error. She put words into God's mouth which He had not spoken: *"...nor shall you touch it, lest you die."* (vs.3) Now, there is no indication in Scripture that they were ever instructed not to touch this fruit, only that they were not to eat it. This may seem a small distinction, but large disasters often have their origin in small errors.

In truth, the only place we are told of this directive prior to it being broken was before Eve's creation, when God instructed Adam thusly (chapter 2, verse 17). So perhaps it was Adam who first added to God's word when He passed it on to Eve. We do not know; we only know that adding to God's directive gave Satan his first claw-hold into wrecking man's vital connection to his Creator.

This same fatal error lives on in our day, as it has down through all the ages before. Going beyond what is written---adding your own pet theologies with no actual basis in sound doctrine--- is a major stumbling block and cause of division. Most church splits are the result of such error. One can even speak truth in such a way as to make it lie, absent its proper context or balance points. Even when one's intention is good, the result cannot help but bring harm. Playing the false prophet by putting words into God's mouth will never end well; there will always be *bitter fruit...*

Quoting the prophet Isaiah (chapter 29, verse 13), the Lord Himself warns us about this error when He rebukes the leading religious figures of His day: *"Hypocrites! Well did Isaiah prophesy about you, saying: 'These people draw near to Me with their mouths, and honor Me with their lips, but their heart is far from Me, and in vain they worship Me, teaching as doctrines the commandments of men.'"* (Matthew 15:7-9) I could step on a lot of religious toes by listing herein a number of these man-made pet doctrines which have crept into certain branches of the church in our day, but we will leave that discussion for another time. Suffice it to say, if you desire to speak for God, make certain that it is His word you speak, and not your own. (See also 1 Corinthians 4:6 and Revelation 22:18-19)

Doubting God's Goodness: This initial claw-hold of adding to God's word opened the door just enough for Satan to slide in his next attack. He accused God of lying, or at least of exaggerating, and of trying to keep something good from Adam and Eve. Here we see the original straw-man… a false accusation with no basis in reality. Surely nothing Eve had ever seen or known of God supported this accusation, yet for some reason it latched onto her anyway. She began to doubt that God really wanted the absolute best for her and Adam. *If there's something He's said 'no' to,* she reasoned, *it must be that He's keeping something good from us.*

In reality, the absolute opposite was the case. When God says 'no', it is to protect us, the same way you would tell your child not to touch a hot stove. But what exactly was this 'forbidden fruit' anyway? What was this 'knowledge of good and evil' which He was trying to protect them from?

In my book ***Sketches and Reflections*** I examine

this topic in detail. In the article "Bitter Fruit" (pages 5-14) I discuss what this fruit represented and why God wanted to spare us from its effects. To state it here in shorthand form, God wanted to spare us from the burden of trying to <u>earn</u> righteousness. This is an impossible task, as the only righteousness we have comes as a free gift from Him. Yet, when we fall short, how easy it is through pride to try to 'make up for it' with God. Our feeble efforts to do so will always fail. We may as well try to jump the Grand Canyon on a pogo stick. And yet we try… and fail. So now we have two failures to make up for… and so on. Do you see the vicious trap here?

<u>The "I" Disease:</u> Now we see the actual commission of sin with which we have been the most familiar. Eve ate of the fruit and gave some to Adam, who ate as well. In doing so, they fell prey to the always-fatal "I" disease. They bought into the lie that they didn't need God, but could be their own gods. Their spiritual vision became darkened, confused, and blurry because they had taken their eyes off of God and focused on self.

 A simple moment of reasoned sanity would have saved them; only God is uncreated. If you are a created being, as all other beings other than God Himself are, it is simply not possible to be your own source. No matter how independent you think yourself, you will always owe your very existence to another.

The law of entropy, in part, states that any energy system separated from a sustaining force will break down and become inert. Stars eventually burn out. Campfires grow cold. If you unplug a lamp from the wall, it goes dark. The same is true of biological systems; sever a branch from its vine and the branch dies. (John 15:4-6)

When Adam and Eve chose to try and be their own 'gods', they were unplugging themselves from the only true source. Immediately, they went dark. (Again, for more details on this, see "Bitter Fruit" in my book *Sketches and Reflections*.) They had separated themselves from God. They had severed the vital connection and violated the very purpose for which they were created, which was for relationship.

Immediately they knew that something was wrong. They knew that they had lost something. Unfortunately, they were still lost in the "I" disease madness and slipped easily from *I can do this myself…* to *I can **fix** this myself!* The glorious covering of light they had been clothed with was gone. They decided to try and replace it with the works of their own hands. A few wrinkly fig leaves proved a poor substitute.

Here we see the full result of the bitter fruit of which they had eaten. They had fully separated themselves from God to the point of actually trying to hide from the all-seeing one. Having unplugged from the source of life and joy, they found themselves plunged into shame, fear, and regret. They had taken their eyes off of their Creator and focused on self and they did not like what they now saw. The glory which once bathed them was now absent because they had severed the vital connection to its source.

Herein is both the true cause and effect of sin. It is "I" focused. It is the opposite of relationship. It is birthed in separation and leads to further separation. When you sin, the burden of guilt and shame serves to focus your eyes ever more intensely on yourself. As when Peter took his eyes off of Jesus in the storm, you begin to sink. The only way out of this death spiral is to have the courage to admit, "I…cannot!" and plug back into the source. Like the prodigal son's father, He is waiting to welcome you home with great joy and gladness.

<u>The Blame Game:</u> Unfortunately, Adam and Eve did not immediately grasp the concept of repentance. If they had, I believe the story may have unfolded somewhat differently. However, when God showed up, they launched into the

blame game. Eve blamed the serpent. Adam blamed Eve, and ultimately he blamed God Himself. "The woman YOU gave me...SHE made me do it... so it's really *your* fault!" he seems to say. (Genesis 3:12).

   Grieved at their fallen, sinful choice, God allows them to begin to bear some of the burden of the separation they have chosen. After all, relationship cannot be forced; it must be chosen. So, He will allow them and their offspring for the next several thousand years to taste the bitter fruit of that separation and decide for themselves if that is really what they want...

   Or perhaps... ever in His heart is the burning fervent desire that they would come to their senses. It is said that you never really know what you have until you lose it. Perhaps, just perhaps, a portion of Adam's descendants will grow to desire that vital connection they once had enough to seek it out once more. The way home was made at Calvary. The cure for that fatal "I" disease is available and it is free, but it must be chosen.

Grace Alone

   Beauty, chaos, creation, decay, order, destruction, rage, serenity, fear, hope, despair and renewal… all tied up together like some great cosmic knot--- this is the world as we have made it, a fabled treasure hidden somewhere within the briar. Every joy fades and every pleasure has a price; everything we build perseveres for but a fleeting season before time and circumstance scatters it to the wind.

   What bitter fruit was spawned in Eden when first we chose to disbelieve. Its dark seed has grown throughout the ages to confuse and choke the simplicity which was always the Sovereign's plan. We sweat and toil and bleed, trying to meet some nameless need, and know too late we never can… for the garden was grace--- and grace alone redeems. It was not for toil, but for love He fashioned man.

Chapter Three
Altar Call

Diligence, faith, virtue, knowledge, self-control, perseverance, godliness, brotherly kindness, love...

This successive list of admirable attributes appears in the opening passages of Peter's second Epistle. (2 Peter 1:5-7) They are noted as traits which should characterize the lives of believers in Christ... those who have become *"partakers of the divine nature, having escaped the corruption that is in the world through lust."* (verse 4) This is not the sole portion of Scripture listing specific positive traits which should be evident within the lives of anyone wearing the title of "Christian". Certainly, these are goals we should all aspire to.

However, given the tenor of the previous chapter, I felt it necessary here to further expound upon and hammer a few points a little closer to home. The fundamental point from which all others will flow is this: These admirable attributes are *fruits*, not *roots*! They are the result of a relationship with Christ, not something which earns that relationship. They are *effect*, not *cause*.

Now, you may claim to know all of this already. Certainly I would assume that anyone who has made it this far into this book possesses some understanding of and bears at least intellectual assent to the fact that it's what Jesus did that saves us and there's nothing we can do to earn it. I would encourage you, however, to go back and scan the previous chapter once more. Really meditate on each section. Contemplate where the least shadow or scar of *Adding to God's Word, Doubting God's Goodness, The I Disease,* or *The Blame Game* may still reside within your heart.

Perhaps you did, many years ago, fully trust in Christ's work on the cross as full payment for your salvation. In that one glorious moment, maybe you did fully grasp the weight of His final words, "It is *finished*..." Yet now it seems that each time you fall short of perfection, you buy into the lie that you somehow have to make up for it with God. Perhaps if you can just feel bad enough about it for a few days... NO! Put that pogo stick away! Drop those fig leaves!

Return once again to that passage in 2 Peter and read a little further. Verse 8 spells out the positive result of walking in the previously mentioned *admirable attributes* of faith; verse 9 gives warning of the negative results of negligence in such. Verse 10 exhorts us to "...*be even more diligent to make your calling and election sure*..." This speaks of the need to solidify your place in Christ by actually living out what you believe. It is of no use to intellectually believe in the power of a parachute to save your life if you don't act on that belief and pull the rip-cord as you plummet toward the ground.

Philippians 2:12-16 and James 2:14-24 both place great emphasis on this same importance of *living out* what you believe. In fact, it is stated with such great emphasis that one could easily see these passages as contradicting the doctrine of salvation by grace alone. However, a careful reading, in context, will reveal their true message: It takes action to turn what you *believe* in your head into what you *know* in your heart. Read a hundred books about welding… and I would still contend that you do not know how to weld until you have actually picked up a torch and practiced it. Read a book about how to train for a marathon and see if that knowledge, unapplied, helps you make it three blocks without losing your breath.

I like to summarize the passage from James in particular as a math equation of sorts:

Information + Application = Revelation

You **see**, you **do**, you **become**…

This is not a question of initial salvation, but of maturing in Christ. It is not a question of being *born again*, but of *growing up*. It's time to get out of diapers.

  Peter concludes his weighty exhortation in verses 12-15 of 2 Peter 1 by first acknowledging that he knows that his audience already has a degree of understanding in these things, but that it is a good idea for them to be reminded from time to time. At the very least, we are all in this same boat. Of all categories of life, it seems that we have the shortest affective memory span for things spiritual. Even if one has fully trusted in Christ alone for salvation, we live in a dark, hostile, and confusing world. This life is a battlefield, awash with lies and distractions. The enemy of our soul floods the airwaves with propaganda and disinformation on a constant basis. We frequently need to be reminded of and be reinforced in clear and simple truth.

  Do you find yourself wasting away hours, days, or even weeks at a time loaded down with the stench of guilt over your latest failure? Those are not *your* hours, days, and weeks; they are Christ's, if you belong to Him! The enemy loves to neutralize Christ's work in the life of His saints. He does so by first seducing them into a pet sin and then going in for the kill. He will hold his boot on the back of your head, keeping you face-down in the mud of shame and condemnation for just as long as you let him get away with it. This is what you must learn, *really* learn, in order to get up out of that mud: You did nothing to earn forgiveness when you first came to Christ; when you blow it now, the same rule applies. Nothing can atone for your sin, then or now, but the shed blood of Christ. The petty little trinkets you would offer in trade are an insult to the price already paid. It would be like offering a dented bottle cap in trade for the Hope Diamond. The only thing He wishes from you is a heart of gratitude and a desire to continue to grow in Him. (See Isaiah 66:1-2, Psalm 34:17-18, Psalm 51:15-17)

***

Or perhaps you fall into a different category---the **unsaved Christian**. What in the world do I mean by that? I mean that you are a church-goer… a devoted do-gooder… a member of the P.T.A., the Ladies Auxiliary Missions Board, a regular soloist in the church choir, or the pastor himself… but you do not truly *know* Christ! Is that even possible?!? Oh, yes… I have known many of you.

You may have grown up in the church, been confirmed, received the special-edition signed Bible, and added your name in big letters to the church membership rolls. You may be able to recite at least a hundred passages from memory and know all kinds of obscure Bible trivia. You may put something in the offering plate every Sunday and do all kinds of good deeds throughout the week. However, you have no genuine, vital connection to Christ. You know a lot about Him, but you do not know Him. You rely not on the cross but on those memorized verses, good deeds, and choir solos to save you.

You may not have realized it until now, but you have religion, not relationship. You are sick, nigh unto death, with that fatal "I" disease. If it remains untreated, you just may hear those dreaded words spoken over you one day, "...*I never knew you; depart from Me...*" (Matthew 7:23)

***

So, then just what exactly is a genuine Christian anyway? I am so very glad that you asked! First, you must realize that a genuine, mature Christian need not be one who necessarily *has it all together*. In many ways the more mature a Christian is, the more readily they will admit that they most decidedly *do not* have it all together and desperately need the One who does, the only one who *has ever* had it all together.

Keith Green, one of the greatest spiritual mentors

of my life, stated the defining characteristic of a true Christian very simply during an altar call at one of his concerts: **"Someone who's <u>bananas</u> for Jesus!"** Relationship is the key. Beyond head knowledge or even perfect obedience, relationship is the key, the foundation; it is what truly matters. Jesus said the same when questioned as to what the most important commandment was: *"Jesus said to him, 'You shall love the Lord your God with all your heart, with all your soul, and with all your mind.' This is the first and great commandment. And the second is like it: 'You shall love your neighbor as yourself.' On these two commandments hang all the Law and the Prophets."* (Matthew 22: 37-40)

Notice the primacy of relationship here? It is both the very foundation of and purpose for everything else. All the good stuff, all of the admirable attributes, spring from the foundation of this relationship and flow back toward it in grateful response. There is no room for condemnation here, which only serves to keep your eyes focused on self, affectively severing relationship.

Neither your guilt nor your good works offered in recompense do anything to earn salvation. However, in the life of a true Christian good works will flow naturally and freely as you stay plugged into the source. As long as you keep the branch of your life attached to the 'true vine', good fruit will follow. It's time to trade in that pogo stick for the bridge built from the blood stained wood of the cross.

***

Now, in speaking at such length on the vain foolishness of allowing oneself to be entangled with the chains of condemnation, please do not assume that I am diminishing the importance of *conviction*! One of the most crucial roles of the Holy Spirit is to bring conviction of sin. When we act in an ungodly manner, we <u>should</u> be grieved! In fact, that grief is evidence that we have been in communion with God; a chief indicator and fruit of relationship is empathy. When we sin, we should feel the grief which God feels over our wrong choices. Every believer should be grateful for such a safeguard. (See Psalm 139:23-24)

The difference between condemnation and conviction lies both in the focus and the fruit. Condemnation keeps us focused on ourselves. We feel bad for how we have blown it. We dwell on…internalize…almost grow to depravedly cherish that pain. Condemnation and shame are self-focused and offer no hope, only guilt.

Condemnation is a leading symptom of the I

disease. It is the currency with which we attempt to pay for something which cannot be purchased, because it has already been paid for. Condemnation is a grimy, dented, rusty bottle cap.

Conviction, on the other hand, is a precious gift. It first makes us aware of the fault, but then points to the solution! It acts like a good doctor, who first informs us of a diagnosis and then immediately points us to the cure. Conviction does not drive us face down into the mud, but lifts our gaze to the cross. Referencing the bronze serpent set up by Moses in Numbers 21, Jesus Himself spoke of this as a foreshadowing of His work on Calvary.

"And as Moses lifted up the serpent in the wilderness, even so must the Son of Man be lifted up, that whoever believes in Him should not perish but have eternal life." (John 3:14-15)

Yes, we feel the pain of having fallen short of His perfection, but in the same moment our gaze is drawn upward to the solution. We are reminded of the grace which comes solely through His work on the cross, not by anything we do to earn it. (See Ephesians 2:1-10) He loves us freely, despite our shortcomings. By this same love He invites us to partner with Him in reaching others.

It is the knowledge of this grace which gives us boldness to look unto Him when we fall short, as each of us will as long as we inhabit this fallen world. Properly embraced, conviction turns our gaze away from our failure and toward the One who loves *without* fail. It turns our gaze from the problem, (our sin) and toward the solution... His marvelous throne of grace. (Hebrews 4:16)

Conviction is the gift of God to turn us back to the right path when we have strayed. When we have taken our eyes off of Christ and severed the vital connection in some way, the conviction of the Holy Spirit is God's way of drawing us back into that right relationship. *Condemnation* is a barrier to relationship. *Conviction* is the bridge which restores it! (See 2Corinthians 7:9-10)

A Cup of Wine

A cup of wine
and a crust of bread
seals the deal…
or so it's said.

Or are these more
than food and drink?
They must mean more…
or so I think.

The body, the blood,
the glory laid low,
paid my full debt;
this much I know.

The shame, the anguish,
the searing pain;
the One who gave all
is worthy to reign.

A Present Help

Do not fear the future,
nor be enslaved to past regrets,
nor doubt the grace in which you stand…
for One,
both infinite and eternal,
holds all of these
within His hand.

Chapter Four
Future Glory

  Hopefully you now possess a clearer understanding of what it actually means to be a follower of Christ, a child of God and co-heir of the coming kingdom. Marvelous, is it not? From the standpoint of these now firmer foundations, let us peer briefly through the veil of ages to come and behold the glory which awaits once time has run its full course. True, what we may perceive while still entrenched within the realm of mortality shall be but the faintest shadow---a fleeting glimpse of the wrapper and the bow---but let us indulge nonetheless.

  Take a few moments to read through the concluding three chapters of the book of Revelation. Make a brief list for yourself of the characteristics of the glorious redemption in store for this very fallen world. Without belaboring the notation of chapter and verse, here are some of the key points I would highlight:

Satan and his forces are imprisoned and no longer able to deceive and tempt mankind.

Born-again believers from every age of history reign with Christ over an unprecedented 1,000 kingdom of peace.

Briefly released from his captivity, Satan makes one last-ditch effort to overcome the Almighty. Christ defeats him without even breaking a sweat and all evil meets final judgement and is put away forever.

Death itself dies.

There is a brand new Heaven, a brand new Earth, and an end to all corruption, sorrow, loss, and decay.

The Bride of Christ is completed and fully purified and the New Jerusalem, our eternal dwelling place, descends from the sky.

Fed by the tree of life, nourished by living waters, and continually bathed by the Shekinah of God, we shall live out an endless future too glorious to be conceived of by mortal minds, yet alone be reduced to written words on paper.

Yes my friend, a truly glorious future awaits those who trust the completed work of Christ. Unfortunately, we cannot live there…yet. Like beholding a distant mountain peak just beyond one which is nearer, we must realize that a valley lies between the two. There is yet a journey ahead before we reach that which burns within our hearts. A crown waits at the finish line, but there is still a race to be run.

Two Men

Two men, living in one skin,
battling for control…
One must die, the other shall fly
to the champion of their soul.
To realms of light, in star-blazed flight
to dance before the throne;
precious gems we are to Him,
who kneel to Him alone.
But first the flame, first the fight…
first the pain, and first the night.
First the race, and then the prize.
First the dust, and then the skies.
Until that day, we yet remain
battling the darkness, overcoming the pain;
two men, living in one skin,
battling for control.

We live very near the completion of the ages, yet we live in a world still very much at war. Though victory is certain, we still must endure ongoing battles against a desperate and savage enemy. The kingdom age approaches…oh, so very near…yet we still live behind enemy lines. Let us take courage in the fact that it is fully within our power to triumph amidst each day's tragedies. *"Yet **in all these things** we are more than conquerors through Him who loved us."* (Romans 8:37)

Charles DeGoulle, Diedrich Bonhoeffer, Oskar Schindler…may we find inspiration in the lives of these great heroes of that human conflict known as World War II. These great men and thousands like them lived lives of great courage and selfless conviction behind enemy lines. Inspired by their example, may we stand boldly against the enemy's schemes, seeking to advance the kingdom as we await the King of Kings.

In doing so, we must hone a keen understanding of the enemy's tactics and how to counter them. Our enemy is clever. He understands our faults, our appetites, and our frailties and knows how to exploit them. Our utter destruction is his highest aim and we must not be ignorant of his schemes.

  We have taken a brief look at the wonders of Eden within the pages of this text, both of the first Eden and of the great restoration to come. It is our enemy's desire to make our lives as much unlike that glory as possible. Every glimmer of hope, peace, and joy we hold within our hearts is an offense to him. He works tirelessly to rob us of anything which bears any resemblance to God's design for our lives. Any glimmer of light we hold within reminds him that the full restoration is on its way…and that is like sand between his teeth.

  We must understand our enemy and his strategies in order to stand against them. If our lives are to bear good fruit for the kingdom, we must both discern and actively stand against the devil's efforts to spoil that fruit. Let us first develop a basic understanding of the enemy's most popular tactics. We shall then examine how to squelch their impact and extinguish these particular fiery darts.

Chapter Five
Arming for Battle

Careful, in-depth study of Scripture is an essential aspect of Christian growth and maturity. We are exhorted to *"Be diligent to present yourself approved to God, a worker who does not need to be ashamed, rightly dividing the word of truth."* (2Timothy 2:15) Examining Scripture in context is crucial. Such observations as who authored a book, who the book was written to, when the book was written, and specific aspects of culture in that time and place can shed a great deal of light on difficult passages. In-depth analysis as to the specific meanings and connotations of words in their original languages may bring much greater understanding as well.

Then there are those like myself who love to delve into the exploration of more hidden treasures... Hebrew, like many ancient languages, is pictographic in nature. Not only do words have very detailed meanings, but the individual letters which make up those words carry meaning themselves. These symbolic meanings of individual letters actually serve to define and bring greater understanding as to the meaning of the words which they make up. Examining these deeper meanings just may revolutionize one's appreciation for the authenticity and authority of Scripture.

All the libraries of the world probably could not hold the totality of this divine wonder. Lifetimes could be spent in daily study of this phenomenon and barely be scratching the surface. However, one small but amazing example may be seen in Exodus 3:14. When Moses asks God who he should say had sent him to lead the people of Israel to freedom, God identifies Himself simple as "I AM"… or, in Hebrew, "Yahweh". What is jaw-droppingly astounding here is the fact that in doing so, He was pointing forward through the ages to the ultimate redemption of the cross.

You see, the holy Name in Hebrew is composed of four letters. In order, these are *yōd, heh, vāv, heh.* The meanings of these letters? I am so very glad you asked! Remember, this is not something which has been recently made up; it is the foundational framework of the Hebrew language from its inception. It is how the written language came to be. So, the meaning of the very Name of God… the Name by which He chose to identify Himself to Moses?

> yōd = "the hand"
> heh = "behold in wonder"
> vāv = "the nail"
> heh = "behold in wonder"

   Truly there are great riches of understanding to be found in scholarly study of the Word. And yet, the more study into these deeper things one does, the more one comes to comprehend an underlying simplicity. In terms of the everyday, practical application of what makes us tick emotionally and spiritually, life is really quite simple. All of us share the same basic needs and desires. We want to love and be loved. We want security and adventure. We want belonging and purpose…we want to matter.

   Understanding and remaining in control of these basic desires is crucially important to victory in this life. The enemy is keenly aware of these universally fundamental human drives. He knows our appetites and takes full advantage of them in his attempts to spoil the fruit of our lives. As in Eden, he seeks to ensnare us through carefully crafted deception. The methods and schemes he devises are innumerable, but they do tend to fall into three main categories: *the bad, the good,* and *the busy.* Let us examine these tactics of the enemy in order to lay hold of the knowledge and conviction to avoid them as much as we are able. No soldier actively engaged in battle expects to make it through his time of service without a scratch. That is not realistic… But if we are aware of the enemy's schemes, we are much less likely to fall prey to them. And we just may inflict some damage upon his forces before it is all over.

Always a Hook

There's always a hook
when the dark one offers
something to entice;
what feeds the hunger
fostered by flesh
carries a pitiful price.

There's always a lie
to lure you back
to that which you forsook;
before you bite
you should consider…
there's always a hook,
always a hook,
always a hook.

The Bad

One of the enemy's prime strategies is to lure us with something we would openly acknowledge as a "bad" thing. This would include behaviors, thoughts, and attitudes which we know are wrong, yet somehow still find appealing. Why is that? If we know that something is harmful, how can we still want it…*so badly?* We know that it will result in pain and shame, and yet still it captivates. Why?

The answer is really quite simple. The enemy utilizes our desires for things God designed for good in order to bring evil. He takes something God created good and corrupts it just enough to bring us harm, yet still remain attractive. We may know that someone sprinkled arsenic on that apple pie over there…but, hey…it's still apple pie. Maybe…maybe just one slice won't hurt. Maybe you're strong enough to handle it. And so you nibble…and the toxin goes to work. The snare is sprung. Satan has played fisherman with a fat, juicy worm and caught another dumb bass…

Many times we fall for this kind of trap through self-justification. We think that we've been good enough that one little compromise won't hurt. *Besides, I really need this,* you think. *I've had it pretty rough lately…so it's ok for me. I just need to have a little fun and blow off some steam. I'm mature enough to handle it...*

And so you conclude that 'the rules' don't apply to you. What you fail to realize is that God is not some kind of cosmic kill-joy; the rules are simply the guard rails which are meant to keep you from going off a cliff. You may think that speed limits don't apply to you, but Trooper Jones will beg to differ. You might want to ignore or just laugh off that "BRIDGE OUT AHEAD" sign back there, but that just may prove to be...your last laugh.

Genesis 1:31 tells us that everything which God made was good. Is there anything in existence which God did not make? Of course not! Please understand this: Whenever God says "No" to something, it is because He sees that it is one of those corruptions of His good creation. All things He created are good, but can be used in a wrong way, or at a wrong time, or can be tainted with impurities by a devious enemy. Apple pie is a wonderful thing, when there's no arsenic involved.

The Good

Another stumbling block for Christians may be ---believe it or not--- doing "good stuff". By this I mean the practice of doing good simply as a matter of external performance. You can do rightly for wrong reasons. You can live right externally without becoming right internally. Let us examine a few scriptures in order to bring clarity to this topic.

In Exodus 24:7 we see Moses presenting the Covenant from God to the people of Israel. Their initial heartfelt response seemed quite encouraging... *"Then he took the Book of the Covenant and read in the hearing of the people. And they said, 'All that the Lord has said we will do, and be obedient.'"*

Even greater encouragement may be hoped for when you examine more closely what is being said here. What is translated as "be obedient" actually has a deeper meaning. It is the Hebrew word *shãmá,* meaning "to come to a full understanding of through obedience". Herein we perceive God's true desire for His children and the reason He desires our obedience. He does not simply want us to be like a dog who rolls-over on command. He desires that we through obedience come to understand and become more like Him. It is about relationship, not performance. He does not simply want us to do, but not understand. He knows that obedience, out of a right heart, leads to positive transformation.

This same principle, I believe, is spoken to from another angle in a Scripture mentioned earlier in this book, James 2:14-24. Man is justified ---his sins forgiven--- by faith alone. However, as James points out, faith is more than intellect. It must be *done*. It must be applied or it does not truly become a part of you. This is the other side of that coin. You can 'do good' without understanding and internalizing that good. But, as James points out, intellectual understanding is worthless if it is not applied. All of the understanding in the world about how a parachute works is of no use if you do not strap it on and pull the rip cord. In verse 22 of this passage, James summarizes this partnership of understanding and action. He asks, *"Do you see that faith was working together with his works, and by works faith was made perfect?"* The Greek word *teleiŏ´o* used here for "perfect" simply means "to be made complete, to accomplish a prescribed goal". Here we see God's end desire regarding our obedience: right action, from a right heart, transforming us into His image.

Unfortunately, this concept never quite solidified within the hearts of His chosen people out there in that desert. They would perform well for a time, but never solidly lay hold of God in their hearts. They knew the *what* with exacting detail, but for the most part never internalized the *why*. Psalm 103:7 tells us that Moses understood God's ways (heart motive) but Israel saw only His acts (external). And so hearts untransformed were not strong enough to override worldly passions. God's hand of correction became necessary again and again in order to turn them back from utter destruction. They focused solely on the external without allowing a change within. They chose religion over relationship.

***

Let us now examine two passages in the New Testament book of Luke. We will begin in Luke 10:38-42. We are told that Jesus entered "a certain village" and a woman named Martha welcomed Him to her home. She greeted Jesus and soon became very busy in serving. (We will examine 'busy' later; for now, let us focus on the 'doing good' aspect of this story.)

She had been trained in the tasks of hospitality nearly from the time she could walk. I am sure she had well-memorized a thousand and one necessary tasks to make someone feel welcome and honored. Excited to have this rabbi under her roof, she paced about quickly (*and gracefully, can't forget gracefully*) as she ticked off one by one the well-established and rehearsed rules of attending to a guest in one's home.

She soon realized, however, that her sister Mary, who was also in attendance, wasn't helping out at all. She was just sitting there…listening to Jesus talk. She hadn't fluffed His pillow once…or refreshed His cup of wine, or brought out the second round of hors d'oeuvres. She was just sitting there chatting with their guest and eating a meal she hadn't even helped to prepare.

Martha soon became too indignant to hold her tongue any longer. Her frantic pace, cold stares, and guilt-inducing sighs just weren't getting through. She finally admonished her guest to order Mary to get off her backside and help out. Jesus' response has become a parable through the ages. While acknowledging Martha's efforts, He actually declared that what Mary was doing was <u>better</u>…and she would not be deprived of it.

You see, Martha was right in the external, at least according to custom, but Mary was right in her heart. Martha was doing all the right "s'posed to" tasks according to the rules of etiquette. However, contrary to modern belief, God is really not all that into rules. As already pointed out, His only real interest in rules is as a means to an end – enabling relationship. He wants us to know Him. Mary had already found that heart of the issue. Martha was still in the shallow end of the pool.

***

Let us now turn a few pages and examine another scene. In Luke 17-18, Jesus is teaching in the villages of Galilee and Samaria on His way to Jerusalem. Along the way He meets, "*…some who trusted in themselves that they were righteous, and despised others."* (Luke 18:9) He tells them a story about two men in the Temple, a cream-of-the-crop Pharisee and…a dirty, rotten tax collector. (*Boo…hiss!* they thought.)

Jesus tells how the Pharisee stood and recounted – with thanks – all of his good works and spotless behavior. He rejoiced in ticking off that well-established list of "s'posed to" accomplishments. The crowd to whom Jesus spoke must certainly have thought that this man would be the hero of the story.

Jesus then turned the crowd's attention to that other guy…the crook, the goofball, the cheater and puppet of the occupying army of Rome. Jesus painted a brief but poignant picture of this man, drenched in shame, acknowledging his sinful state before God. He beat his chest and called out for mercy. *'Fat chance!'* the crowd thought as they sneered in pride. *Someone should toss that loser out on his ear!*

Jesus rocked the crowd by announcing that it was the tax collector, not the Pharisee, who was justified before God that day. Once again, we see that it is the <u>heart</u> which God is truly after, not external performance. Doing good only has value if it helps to make you good.

The Busy

Honest labor is a necessary component of life on this little blue ball. Under the right conditions it can bring a good measure of purpose and even enjoyment to our lives. It was meant to be a frame work around which fellowship is built. It has been a part of God's plan for mankind since the beginning.

Unfortunately, like everything else it has fallen far from its original state since the days of Eden. Our first parents were given just two tasks to carry out: garden and make babies! My poor little mortal mind cannot grasp how they fell for the line that there was something better they were missing out on!

But fall they did. And with that fall, labor became much more laborious. Life would now be a struggle. Nothing would come easy again. Strangely, after a few millennia of grudgingly enduring this struggle, a large segment of mankind has become addicted to it. They have grown to love it. They are enamored with the hamster wheel and what was originally seen as a curse has become the new drug… and millions are hooked.

They proudly wear labels like "workaholic" and "multi-tasker" (which to me simply means that you never finish anything you start…you just keep starting something new.) Now, Scripture does not exalt slothfulness and neither do I. However, neither does it condone deification of self, and that is exactly what this drug does. It wraps the whole person…the identity and feeling of self-worth…around what is supposed to be a minor component of one's life. Friends, family, sanity…all become sacrificed upon the altar of achievement. The only thing which matters is that next fix, the next rung on the ladder of success. The end result is a burned-out life full of regret. Like all drugs, it promises fun and fulfillment but leaves you empty, broken, and lonely.

***

Others use this drug not in the pursuit of status, but in order to avoid something else. When there is something wrong in our bodies, God allows pain in order to make us aware of the issue so that it may be attended to. Drugs are often prescribed to help deaden excessive pain, but if one does so without addressing the cause, they are a fool.

Far too many people in our world use work as a way to deaden or ignore the pain of some area where God desires to bring healing. They seek to drown or crowd out the pain in any way possible without addressing the issue. I have been guilty of this at times. It is far too easy to slip into the mode of *If I can just stay busy enough, I won't have to think about that…* But a wound which is not dealt with will only grow worse and cause much greater harm in the end. Do not fall for the trap of staying too busy to think---too busy to feel.

"Always busy" is a favorite tactic of the enemy to empty our lives of anything of true worth. Busyness is a worthless counterfeit of fruitfulness, but it is oh so easy to fall for. This is especially true for those of us in full-time Christian service. There is always…always something more which needs to be done. To-do lists are a daily way of life; we are heavy consumers of sticky-notes. We have a different term for a 40-hour work week: vacation!

Yes, we are often simply too busy. If we do not stay alert to this danger, we can find ourselves burning a whole lot of time but producing very little fruit. That, my friend, is a wasted life. May we all, both in Christian service and in secular employment, learn to cultivate a proper balance between work and rest. We may just find that if we *do* a bit less and *fellowship* a bit more, we will actually be far more fruitful in work and in ministry. In the next chapter we will discuss a simple framework for addressing this and avoiding the snares of *the bad, the good,* and *the busy.*

Life

Life… real life is a hay field, yielding to God's breath. It is not found in those harder things: concrete, and plaster, and asphalt… vain attempts at significance and permanency which without fail pass away in but a few seasons, victims of a softer hand.

Real life, everlasting life is found in that which bends and bows, and dances and dies, and rises with the breeze once more. It is in that simplicity which hides a billion details, ever changing, yet eternal… birth, death, and renewal, created and sustained by a master hand.

Serenity

To sleep away
a summer's day
in meadows warm and fair
beneath the cloak
of aspen and oak
so ignorant of care
that passing hours
like fading flowers
expire unaware.

Chapter Six
Grasping for Eden

So just how do we live with focus and fruitfulness in a blurry and chaotic world? What are the keys to cultivating a life of true purpose and simple joy like we were meant to have? How do we return to Eden?

Anyone with even a tenuous grip on reality should realize that the fullness of this proposition is simply not possible under the current world system. Paradise is only possible under the direct leadership of the Prince of Peace. Until He returns to establish His glorious kingdom, we can only know a shadow of that glory. Too many of our fellow humans live apart from His divine example altogether and, in truth, we all fall miserably short. Fullness of glory will only find its revelation in the ages to come.

However, those of us called by His name are to live out kingdom principles in this *present* age. We are called to occupy the land and to represent the King's authority and character until He comes. Only He will fully restore Eden, but each of us can and should cultivate a little patch of it, to the best of our ability, within our own lives. Let us examine a few principles for doing so.

Many of Jesus' parables spoke directly to the agrarian society of His time. Mankind's relationship with God began in a garden and will culminate there as well. Despite nearly miraculous advances in technology and industrialization, agriculture continues to be central to the human experience. After all, you can't eat *computer* chips! So let us follow the example of the Master Gardener and build a framework of understanding around a few simple agricultural concepts: *Prune, Feed, Water,* and *Weed...*

Prune

Take a moment to consider the words of Jesus in John 15:1-2. *"I am the true vine, and My Father is the vinedresser. Every branch in Me that does not bear fruit He takes away; and every branch that bears fruit He prunes, that it may bear more fruit."* Jesus speaks here in relation to grape vines, but similar principles apply to most any fruit bearing vine or tree. In order to be fruitful, it must be pruned.

Pruning involves more than just one process. Initially, any diseased or damaged branches are removed, along with any which show no sign of developing fruit-producing buds. Obviously, to allow these branches to remain would divert needed resources away from those branches which show the potential for bearing fruit. Leaving them in place might make for a grander looking, more impressive vine or tree, but would result in much less fruit and of an inferior quality.

   This principle speaks directly to our lives as Christians. What is there in your personal life or ministry which, although grand-looking and showy, bears no fruit? Is there a ministry position which you have taken on simply because it will look good on your resume… or Facebook page? Is there any spotlight-seeking in your sacred service?

   What activities are you involved with simply to fill time or because *someone had to?* Have you taken on so many of these *branches* that the only answer you ever have for, "How have you been?" is, "Busy…"? Do you regularly review your calendar hoping to find an open slot of time to eat, sleep, or tie your shoes?

   Please remember one of our prime principles: ***Busy*** does not equal ***fruitful!*** Take an honest inventory; how many of your *branches* are currently bearing any fruit? Which ones may have borne fruit in years past, but no longer do? Which <u>are</u> bearing fruit, but of an inferior quality because they lack the energy and resources being diverted to the fruitless branches? Sit down at your kitchen table with God and make an honest inventory.

Make a written list and commit to action. It just may be time to take out the loppers.

***

Another aspect of pruning comes into play when fruit has begun to form. This is the process of thinning. Sometimes a branch can be *too* fruitful. Though lots of fruit begins to form, the experienced vinedresser knows that leaving it all in place is not a wise choice. To do so would bring multiple problems.

Firstly, to divide the available resources among too much fruit would result in stunting the growth of all of the fruit. If you want big, beautiful, delicious grapes (or apples, pears, etc…) you must remove some of the initial growth. You must thin in order for essential resources to produce the best possible crop in that which remains.

Too much fruit can also spell trouble by overloading branches. Excessive weight may be compensated for by tying or propping branches, but sometimes this is simply not good enough, especially if a strong wind or heavy rain strikes. As strain increases, the overloaded branch may crack and all of its fruit be lost.

Well, if most of your fruit looks stunted and you

feel like you are starting to crack under the weight, perhaps you should consider Jesus' words in Matthew 11: 28-30... *"Come to Me, all you who labor and are heavy laden, and I will give you rest. Take My yoke upon you and learn from Me, for I am gentle and lowly in heart, and you will find rest for your souls. For My yoke is easy and My burden is light."*

If the yoke you are laboring under runs far-afield from *"easy...*and *light..."*perhaps, just perhaps you are pulling on the wrong yoke. Maybe it's not one He gave you, but one you picked out for yourself. If God is not in a ministry project with you because it is not a yoke He designed for you, is it any wonder the burden seems heavy and drags you down?

Even if it seems a "good thing", it just could be a good thing He designed for someone else to accomplish. Do not fall into the trap of having to do every good thing which comes along. To do so robs others of the opportunity which may have been their God-ordained yoke. Every yoke involves effort, but if it does not bring you joy, perhaps it is because it belongs to someone else. Do not rob others of their fruitfulness by usurping their opportunity to serve. Thin out those fruitful branches and lay down any yoke which the Spirit did not lead you to.

***

A final round of pruning comes in the late fall, following harvest. Any *suckers* which have developed over the summer, along with some of those branches which bore good fruit, are removed. This is done for a number of reasons, especially in orchards.

Proper shape of and spacing between branches allows greater penetration of sunlight to lower branches. It also greatly aids in ease and efficiency of harvesting the fruit. Great care is taken to guide the development of each individual branch along with the tree as a whole. Letting go of a small portion of the branches which bore good fruit actually serves the well-being of the whole tree.

In like manner, there are occasional aspects of our lives and ministries which, although they have born good fruit, need to be laid down or passed on to others. God is the Master Designer and the only one with the wisdom to prune us for the good of our whole being. We need to learn to take up only those yokes He leads us to. We also need to learn the grace to lay down those particular good works when He so leads.

There are *seasons* in life and ministry. There are

times when He calls us to rest from one labor before He leads us to the next. There are times He calls us to bring a particular ministry project only to a certain level because that is where He has designed it to be passed on to another. It is someone else's God-ordained yoke to take it farther on. Remember, one may plant and another water, but the work is God's. He is the foreman; we are just fellow-workers. (see 1Corinthians3:4-8) Do not allow the blessing of being called to serve to become an idol in your heart. Yes, the ministry you perform in service to the King is valuable; it actually helps to shape eternal destinies. However, your identity should be in Christ Himself, not in the work which you do for Him. God loves and desires YOU, not just what you do.

Feed

Take a moment to read 2Timothy 2:15 once again. Imagine the tone in Paul's voice and really hear the earnestness as he exhorts the young man Timothy. Now consider also his words in an earlier letter... 1Timothy 4:13-16. Read also Psalm 119:15-16, Hebrews 5:12-14, and Joshua 1:8.

What theme do you see developing in these passages? These are just a few examples of the many portions of Scripture which exhort us to not neglect to "feed" upon the riches of God's word. We are exhorted to *dwell upon, meditate, consider...* to metaphorically feed upon His written word. This refers, of course, to the practice of intellectual study.

Consider especially the passage from Hebrews, which speaks of the "meat" of the word. This passage exhorts us to take the time to probe the deeper things of God through careful, in-depth study of His word. This goes beyond the "milk" of the elemental truths which first drew us to Christ. Now, milk is essential...it has its place...but meat is crucial to maturing in our walk. If you are a thirty year old and still drink from a bottle or sippy-cup, something is wrong. We should be eager to put forth the effort to grow in deeper understanding and maturity.

However, please understand that intellectual study simply for its own sake is of little eternal significance. God will not be impressed with how many cerebral folds you were able to acquire during your three-score and ten years upon this earth. Knowledge simply for the sake of knowledge is empty and pretty pointless. Solomon states this case with a hint of ironic morose is Ecclesiastes 12:12. *"...Of making many books there is no end, and much study is wearisome to the flesh."*

However, knowledge which is applied toward a desired end is wisdom. God is not interested in us memorizing facts, figures, and dates. He wants us to know His word because that is one of the chief ways we come to know **Him**. He wants us to know and apply His word so that we can, like Moses, come to **understand** Him---to know His heart, not just His actions. (Psalm 103:7)

It is also important to grow in our intellectual understanding of the word in order to safeguard against deception. The devil knows the word better than most Christians. He constantly seeks to pervert and twist it in order to deceive and lead astray. Unbelievably, he even tried this devious tactic against the Living Word Himself! (see Matthew 4:1-11)

Through regular, concentrated times of in-depth study we send our spiritual roots deeper into the solid ground of real understanding. Original language studies, ferreting out historical and cultural context, and even biographical studies can all shed new light upon and flesh out fuller meanings within scriptures which we may have read dozens of times before. The deeper our roots grow in this fuller understanding, the more able we will be to withstand the storms of deception. And any orchardist or vineyard owner knows that deeper roots means better fruit.

So feeding upon God's word is a crucial aspect of Christian growth. More in-depth study, learning to chew on the meat of the Word, is especially important to learning our Father's heart. It strengthens our roots and leads us nearer Eden's gate. It is possible to simultaneously grow in both intellectual prowess and childlike wonder. That is, in fact, quite like our Father. He both dreamed up and designed the very building blocks of matter...and the spots on a ladybug's back.

Water

"O God, You are my God; early will I seek You; my soul thirsts for You; my flesh longs for You in a dry and thirsty land where there is no water." Psalm 63:1

Water is just as important to growth and health as food, if not more so. After all, one can survive much longer without food than without water. You can go for months without food, but only a few days without water. As food is herein equated with the intellectual study of God's word, let us consider water to represent our emotional connection to God...our heart relationship to the Father...the intuitive aspect of our nature.

Certainly the spiritual food of intellectual study is important to our growth. We may just come to see, however, that the water of our emotional and intuitive connection is even more vital. An intellectual understanding about women (if such a thing were possible…) would bring you very little success or joy in a marriage relationship on its own. It is the heart-to-heart, intuitive understanding which is more vital. And so it is with our relationship to God, who is much more concerned with our heart than with our head. May we learn to appreciate and walk in the intuitive as readily as we lean upon intellect. We study to know *about* God, but we must fellowship — soak in His presence — to truly *know* Him.

In order to grow in intellect, we must immerse ourselves in times of focused study. If we wish to grow in the intuitive, we must learn perhaps a more difficult discipline. We must learn to immerse ourselves in times of *focused repose*. We must learn to shut off all the noise of the world and demands of work and ministry and to embrace the practice of sanctified solitude.

Jesus Himself, despite the demands of ministry (or perhaps *because of*), often withdrew from the crowds and sought out a place of solitude. (See Mark 6:46 and Luke 5:16) He knew that all of the work of ministry He could accomplish would mean nothing if He Himself missed the whole point—fellowship with the Father. His priority was always focused upon maintaining that relationship.

As with Him, maintaining and expanding upon that relationship must be the true aim and focus of our service. If ministry does not spring forth *from* and feed back *into* that relationship, our so-called ministry has become an empty work of the flesh. It is wood, hay, and stubble and of no eternal value. (1 Corinthians 3:12-15) Times of prayer and focused solitude with the Father awaken within us the capacity to serve, not just *work*, which is the inferior concept.

I began my life of full time ministry by training and serving for a little over three years at Last Days Ministries in east Texas. One account shared by a teacher in my schooling there had a huge impact on my early spiritual growth and continues to impact me to this day. He shared with the class about a time in prayer which pierced his heart, igniting a new passion for the Father.

One morning he simply felt like, instead of bringing a list of needs before the Throne, he should ask God what was on **His** heart. Certainly we are told to bring our cares to the Lord, but this day he simply felt like he should ask God what concerned *Him*. He came to listen, not just to ask. He wanted to know how he could minister to the Father...how he could bless the Lord's heart.

This man of God was totally caught off guard by the Lord's response. It hurt in a *beautiful* way, granting new depth and insight into the true heart of Father God. He recounted how that, deep in his spirit, he heard six little words, saturated with a nostalgic pathos: ***"I miss my walks with Adam..."***

In a profound way, he came to understand the true heart of God for His children. He is not looking for what we can do for Him; He just wants us. He is love...and love is not purchased. God's central desire is not that we serve Him, but that we learn to know Him — and love Him — in return.

Beginning from that crucial foundation of relationship, it *is* true that we shall grow in our desire to please Him. That is true of any relationship. We want to serve and please the object of our affection. We get joy from bringing joy to others. We must, however, never confuse cause and effect. We do not serve God in order to earn His love, but *because* of His love! Do not ever forget that relationship — knowing God — is the true foundation of any service in ministry. What we do in life and ministry is of no value whatsoever unless it is rooted in His love.

So what are some of the ways in which we can really connect with God in our times of solitude? Just being alone is not the point, after all, but being alone *with God*. How do we tune our hearts into His and truly connect on that intuitive level? How do we *focus* our *repose*?

***

One of my favorite ways to spend focused time with God is simply to get out into nature with Him. Romans 1:20 and many other scriptures tell us that there is much we can know of God simply by observing His creation. Numerous aspects of both His character and personality can be seen in the grand and majestic, as well as the tiny and obscure.

Let your eyes feed wisdom to your heart as you take in the full splendor of a mist-shrouded mountain range…a lonely beach…or star-strewn summer evening. Stretch out in a sunny meadow and go on a treasure hunt; seek out and marvel at the myriad of tiny jewels hiding under the grass — wildflowers so small that only a miniscule fraction of humanity will ever even realize that they exist. Now consider that the same God who stretched out the endless sky above crafted those tiny blooms in all of their miniaturized detail as well. What does this tell you about the limitless nature of His power, His love, His creativity, and childlike wonder? Do you begin to see your Father's heart in all of these wonders, both immense and miniscule?

***

Bible study can and should be a part of this kind of time alone with God as well. However, see that you focus primarily on hearing and seeing with your heart. Leave those Greek lexicons aside for the time being and read His word like a love letter.

Spend some time in the Psalms and those *redletter* portions of the New Testament. Allow analytical dissection to take a back seat for the moment and focus on hearing the Father's heart in what you read. Read slowly through Psalm 78 and see if you cannot help but touch upon the frustration and broken heart of God over a stubborn and rebellious people. In order to really know someone, you must be willing to experience the fellowship of their suffering. (Philippians 3:8-11) As you spend time in God's word, be still and really open your heart to His. You may touch upon a measure of pain there, but you will also find a level of blessing and intimacy which others will never know.

***

There are a few books outside of the Bible which I would also recommend as part of your heart-to-heart times with God. Many Christian books aim more for the intellect, which has its place, but here we are more concerned with opening the eyes of your heart. One such book does that better than any other I have ever read. This is **The Divine Romance**, by Gene Edwards. Simply put, it is a narrative account of all of time and eternity…told from God's point of view. In my opinion, this masterpiece of literature may hold more of the true heart of Scripture than any other book outside of Scripture itself.

Being at heart a poet, I would of course recommend books of Christian poetry and prose as well. To be brutally honest, there is a lot of modern Christian poetry out there — very little of it very good from an artistic or literary standpoint. I can recommend the writings of Ruth Bell Graham, the late wife of Billy Graham. I have read and enjoyed some of her works, including *Clouds are the Dust of His Feet*.

Of course, one can consider classical poets as well, such as John Milton, William Blake, Geoffrey Hill, or my personal favorite, Robert Frost. In fact, most of the poets of renown were believers. Much of their writing, though exceptional, is rather formal and aims more at the intellect, however. Again, it has its place, providing you steer the intellect toward opening the understanding of your heart.

One closing note on this particular topic: If you are interested in checking out some of my books of poetry, prose, and short writings, see the list of such titles at the conclusion of this book.

***

Let us now discuss one final method of connecting with God on an intuitive level, the practice of journaling. Many people keep a diary in which they record their thoughts and reflections each day. This is not what I speak of here, however. Journaling is quite a different experience.

Put simply, journaling is not writing down *your* thoughts, but God's as He speaks them to you. Now, most people are going to begin avoiding you or at least looking upon you with misplaced pity if you start going around saying that you've heard God speak… The fact remains, however, that Jesus said, **"My sheep hear my voice…"** in John 10:27.

I am most certainly not saying that all believers regularly converse with the Almighty and hear audibly His voice with ears of flesh. That is, in fact, an exceedingly rare occurrence. It is a profoundly wonderful experience, one which I have been privileged with on three occasions, but is not the sole qualifier for *hearing His voice*. God speaks in many ways, usually in a very still, quiet, internal kind of voice. If you are a believer, it is a voice you have heard, whether or not you fully realized that it was Him speaking at the time.

You can, however, learn to recognize the voice of God and to discern it as distinct from all of the other internal voices. You can do this in much the same way that you learn to recognize the voice of a relative or close friend on the telephone. Like any loving parent, He wants to both hear from and speak to His children. We simply need to learn to listen. The practice of journaling is a vital aid in this pursuit.

The first step is to come to God with a clean heart. Confess and forsake any sin in your life. Unconfessed sin and its accompanying burden of guilt and shame is sure to be a barrier to open communication. Just look at Adam and Eve in the garden; they felt the shame of disobedience and hid from God. If you want to hear from God, you must walk in the light and allow Him to remove any barrier to fellowship. (See 1 John 1:7).

Now, simply be still in His presence and know that He wants to speak to you. Turn off the phone, the television, the computer...and actively resist any other distractions which seek to encroach. Have a pen in hand and a blank piece of paper or two in front of you and listen for His voice. Ask Him to speak and do not be in a hurry.

Expect Him to speak in first-person, as anyone else you were conversing with would. When you sense Him begin to speak, let it flow. Write down whatever comes, without analyzing it at that time. You can weigh it later, making sure that what you believe you've heard lines up with Scripture — an important safeguard. God will never speak anything which conflicts with His word.

Sometimes, the Lord may only speak a simple phrase or even a single word, which He will then expound upon at a later time. He may speak a Scripture reference, or give you a message of encouragement or exhortation. Whatever the case, as you regularly spend time in this manner, your level of intimacy with Him will grow exponentially. As you learn to recognize His voice in this way, you will also see His hand in your daily life in new ways and many of your former anxieties will fade. His voice speaks peace.

Weed

I am sure that you have by now well noted how we have established *agriculture* as the metaphor of choice within the pages of this treatise on spiritual growth. Rightly so, I should think, as our chief aim herein has been the examination of a return to simplicity and refocusing upon the fundamentals of life as it was originally meant to be lived. After all, contrary to popular modern euphemism, gardening is actually ***the world's oldest profession!*** (See Genesis 2:15)

Bearing this in mind, let us now conclude with an examination of every gardener's arduous necessity. I speak of weeding. Though never a truly pleasant task, one must take regular action to deal with those unwanted little monsters which spring up on a regular basis, sapping strength away from the fruitful crop we have labored to produce.

If not regularly dealt with, weeds will overshadow, entangle, and even strangle the crop. Even if they do not totally destroy the intended agricultural pursuit, fruit will be limited, if present at all. Ideally, weeding should be done quite regularly, even daily. After all, the earlier one deals with a weed, the shallower its root and less likely that it has had the chance to spread seed, thus becoming a bigger problem.

While learning to deal with the weeds in our own lives, it would be beneficial to foster an understanding of where they originate. After all, those of us who aspire to live a life which could reasonably be regarded as "Christian" **want** to do *right*... So why is it that we find ourselves infested with weeds of *wrong* on such a regular basis?

Well, I have heard tell that some guy who authored a major chunk of the New Testament struggled with this very dilemma on occasion. Just take a stroll through the seventh chapter of the book of Romans. See if you don't recognize that particular experience of exasperated frustration within those passages. Paul had his weeds to deal with, the same as any of us.

In addition to rejoicing in the Master Gardener's tremendous grace, the persecutor-turned-apostle begins to hint at the source of this predicament in chapter eight. You see, man (like the God in who's image he is created) is a three-part being. We are a trinity. When you look into a mirror, you see your physical body — that which is visible to the eyes of flesh. What you do not see, though they are just as real and present, are the mind and spirit.

We are a three-part being. When we are born again, our spirit is immediately redeemed. It is immediately made right with God and transformed into its new eternal state…salvation. (Ephesians 2:8-9)

Please note, however, that we are more than spirit! We have a mind and inhabit a physical body. Neither the mind nor the body enters its eternal, redeemed state at the moment the spirit does. The mind begins at that moment a life-long trek towards redemption; it is a journey which is walked out, with great effort, on a daily basis. Every choice we make either helps or hinders our journey on this road. It is a frequently arduous process of growth with no short cuts, only wise choices and hard work. (See Ephesians 4:20-32, Psalm 119:11, Romans 12:2, 2 Peter 1:5-11)

Our physical body, born in an already fallen state, will not know its redemption until after it has been cast into the ground like a seed. No matter how carefully you eat and how regularly you exercise, should the Lord tarry, you are going to get wrinkly! You are going to lose your hair, your eyesight, your hearing…and eventually, your pulse.

And in every moment until that final flutter of cardiac contraction, you will be subject to impulses which arise from dwelling in a fallen fleshly abode. You will do battle with appetites and desires which seek to reign supreme over your mind and spirit. You will strain to exercise control over driving forces elemental to the physical aspect of our nature, still quite removed from the glory of its original design. This is the nature of that internal war with which we are all too familiar.

   This battle will continue in each of us until the seed is cast…and finally born anew. Corruption must put on incorruption; that which has fallen shall arise in new glory. Though it is for now diminishing day by day, the flesh **will** know its redemption. (1 Corinthians 15:42-58, 2 Corinthians 4:16-18)

***

   Now that we understand a bit of why we face so many weeds — that two-thirds of our make-up is yet to be truly redeemed — let us take a look at the process of dealing with those weeds which infest the garden of our lives. We will examine a few basic categories of weeds. Not all weeds operate in the same way. A better understanding of individual weeds and the ways in which they infest will lead to better strategies in recognizing and dealing with them.

The most obvious weeds—the ones which we are most likely to immediately identify as such—are blatant outward sins. These are generally seen as the *don'ts* we all probably remember from Sunday school. Topping the list are such things as drunkenness, immorality, stealing, lying, violence…perhaps even chewing gum in class, depending upon the strictness of your particular denominational background!

Most of us who are Christians, or at least have been part of a church for a while, are probably pretty good at keeping the majority of these particular weeds in check. However, many times we have done nothing more than cut them off at ground level. Far too often we have done little or nothing to deal with the **roots** of these behaviors. Read through the **fifth chapter of Matthew** and take careful note of how keenly Jesus focuses in on the heart issues from which these external sins originate.

This is especially emphasized in regards to the issues addressed in verses 21-32. You don't sleep around or make it a habit to actually carry out that grisly murder you dreamed up for that guy who cut you off in traffic? Great! But God looks deeper. Pastor What's-his-name may be impressed, but God is not. He sees the thoughts and attitudes from which outward sins emerge. He knows that as long as these roots remain, you are under the enemy's influence.

According to this Scripture, guilt in your heart is just as damning as guilt of commission. So you must be careful to allow the Holy Spirit to deal with any *bitter roots* in your heart. Many times there are issues which we would never even recognize. We are very good at lying to ourselves and self-justifying. A man or woman of true courage will make a regular habit of asking the Holy Spirit to turn His spotlight of conviction upon their heart. They will want to be made aware of any of these roots which need to be dealt with. A heart which has determined to be obedient is a heart which will hear. (See Jeremiah 17:9-10, Psalm 139: 23-24)

***

Having just discussed the roots of sinful attitudes and thoughts, let us now turn our attention to another kind of weed which may hide just under the surface…one which may also send its strangling roots deep into our hearts. I speak of spiritual and emotional wounds. Like the formerly mentioned weeds, these may present little outward sign of their presence, although the opposite may very well be the case. You have probably heard it said, "Hurting people hurt people."

Broken families, bullying, rejection, physical and sexual abuse, loneliness… all of these far too common elements of modern life cannot help but leave deep scars and bitter entanglements. The enemy of our souls delights in fostering these destructive patterns and sending toxic, strangling roots deep into the hearts and minds of people too young or already wounded to understand or resist. These roots become his barbed-wire marionette strings which he uses to control and enslave in an ongoing celebration of misery and hopelessness.

Even when we have become born again, there may be significant remnants of these roots left to deal with. Depression, anger, fear, a lack of self-worth…these and many other destructive residues of the enemy's scheme may have simply become well ingrained reflexive impulses. A great deal of time and sometimes painful soul-surgery may be required before a significant measure of freedom is achieved.

I have dealt with this kind of recovery from wounding for many years. At the time of this writing, I am 47 years of age. I still carry very vivid memories of both physical abuse and emotional abandonment from over four decades ago. My natural father having recently passed, I now feel open — at least a little — to discuss this in public.

The physical and emotional mistreatment I experienced from my natural father caused some definite consternation for my adoptive dad. He just could not understand why when he would speak sternly, raise his hand, or walk in my direction, I would flinch, duck, and shield my face. He had never been backhanded by his dad for spilling a glass of water. I had. He had no memory, as I had, of plodding down the stairs as a six year old, carrying a baseball bat, to try and defend my mother from my drunk and angry father.

I know that the way I often reacted around my adoptive father hurt him, and even embarrassed him in public… But I quite literally could not help myself. There were very real emotional wounds from physical abuse which took years to resolve.

Another one of these roots took many years longer to be dealt with to a significant degree. My natural father never paid child support — not a nickel. I realize that this was his attempt to get at my mom, but it obviously affected us kids. What truly hurt me, however, was the final legal resolution of this issue.

I vividly recall the sunny summer afternoon in Nebraska when he called from Oregon. I overheard the heated discussion wherein my natural father finally agreed to allow us kids to be adopted by the man we called "Randy-Dad" and to relinquish all visitation rights. What truly hurt was that he only agreed to this in exchange for my mother agreeing to never pursue any claim for unpaid child support.

Though I was ok with this arrangement on one level; I really had no desire at that time to ever see him again; I felt very much abandoned. I felt as if I had been sold. We truly meant so little to him that keeping his money was more important. Some very destructive roots began to take hold in my nine year old heart that day.

Over the following decades I battled ongoing bouts of fear over financial provision, especially as I looked toward the completion of high school. I had been abused by and then both emotionally and financially abandoned by my natural father. I can assure you, that leaves scars…and bitter roots.

Now take a moment and ponder something with me… How do you think that God brought me through this to healing? Did I come into a large inheritance from a wealthy oil-tycoon uncle? Did I win the lottery on my eighteenth birthday? Did

Ed McMahon actually show up at my door, just like in all of those old television commercials?

No…on all counts. God called me to be a missionary. Basically since I graduated high school I have served in full-time ministry and missions. For those of you unfamiliar with this lifestyle, it is not one which is heavily populated with millionaires. I have shared a bedroom with eight other single guys. I have lived on three meals a day, a bed, and twenty dollars a month, out of which I tithed to the church I attended. I have at times had less than thirty dollars left to my name. Without dwelling for too long on this subject, God has done soul surgery on me over the past decades—at every turn showing Himself to be the loving Daddy I was deprived of in the natural.

I have a wife of nearly twenty-five years and a wonderful seventeen year old son. Though we have never had a large surplus, we have never lacked anything which was a true need. I have also done a good bit more traveling than many wealthier Americans and have had friends from fifty-six nations so far, having traveled in five. In faithfully providing for me and my family all of these years, God has brought a real measure of healing. He has come a long way in digging out those bitter roots caused by pain too deep to express in words. He is well on the way to bringing true freedom to this heart which was so fearfully bound. He can do the same for you.

***

One final weed which we will discuss is that of time-eaters. I have had friends who died young. I also currently have friends whom I have a hard time believing are still alive and kicking. None of us knows the measure of our days. Time is not the sole determining factor in how much fruit our lives will produce, but we are responsible to use the time we have on this earth wisely. It is a resource; like any resource with which we are entrusted, we are responsible for how we invest it…or fritter it away.

Surely recreation has a place in our lives and, as we have discussed, simple times of solitude are a tremendous benefit in getting to know God. He is no harsh taskmaster, demanding that every waking moment be scheduled and accounted for in a ledger…filed in triplicate on a weekly basis. It is perfectly ok to have down times and even to enjoy occasional distractions from more weighty matters of life and ministry. It is healthy. It is even unbalanced and ultimately destructive to not do so.

When these enjoyable distractions become controlling habits, however, there is a problem. How many of you have a television program which you simply *cannot* miss? How many of you do not feel complete unless you are first in line to buy the newest so-called smart phone? Have you begun to shape your identity around some form of entertainment like music or movies? Any hard-core Trekkies out there? Or perhaps you are just a little too into sports, popular culture, or —gasp— Facebook?

Ok, so I love watching cheesy old 1950s science fiction movies and television shows. I also really appreciate the...um...sophisticated social commentary of animated series like **The Tick** and **Angry Beavers**. I occasionally like to read really old novels or flip through hunting or fishing magazines. I enjoy video games. Life in ministry can be especially busy just in day to day getting stuff done and there is no harm in a measure of unwinding in pursuits which are not necessarily "spiritual".

What can be harmful, however, is when these very human things become too much a need or begin to shape our personalities more than our time with God. When they become a controlling factor, something is wrong. Have you ever sensed God putting something on your heart, and put

Him on *hold* because you were in the middle of the latest episode of your favorite show? "Ooooo, hold that thought, God! I'll get back to you on the next commercial….promise!" You have just shown God where your true affections lie, and it's not with Him.

Keith Green recorded a timeless, highly convicting song on the album *So You Wanna' Go Back to Egypt*. It's title alone pretty much sums up this topic: "You Love the World (and You're Avoiding Me)". I have often thought that it would be a fun project to record a slightly modernized version, with updated lyrics:

My Word sits there, upon your desk,
but you love YouTube and Facebook the best.
You prefer the light of your PC,
You love Netflix
and you're avoiding Me!

Listen to the real, original song and see where you might sense a level of conviction. If you do not own the album, hey, it's on YouTube! It is ok, even healthy, to enjoy innocent distractions, as long as they do not become addictions. If they unseat God from the throne of your heart, they have become an idol, and should be uprooted. If any pursuit eats up too much of your time, energy, and focus, it is time to cut ties and put it aside. Listen to the voice of the Holy Spirit when He brings conviction over one of these weeds of time-eaters and re-evaluate your use of this resource. Otherwise, you just may find yourself with a life full of weeds and precious little fruit.

I still remember Pastor Tracy Hanson of Community Christian Fellowship in Garden Valley, Texas preaching a message on this very topic nearly thirty years ago. For a good part of the sermon, I was honestly having a difficult time following what he was getting at. Then the Holy Spirit spoke directly to me, bringing a tremendous rush of clarity to my mind: *The devil builds more amusement parks than prisons...*

Allow that concept to soak in for a while...and take an honest look at where you may make better use of the resource of time in knowing and serving the Father. How might you focus better on the things which *really* matter?

"To know God and to make Him known" is the official motto of Youth With A Mission. I cannot think of a better life purpose statement than that. I cannot think of a more worthy goal to focus one's life upon. I hope that you have been blessed by this book, and that it has in some measure helped *you* in this very pursuit.

Discernment

If you want to hear God, listen to the rain as it dances on autumn leaves. Listen to the thunder as it echoes down mountain canyons…as it argues between the peaks.

Listen to the little streamlets as they pick their way down hillsides and dive from rocky cliffs. Listen as heavy branches laden with moss let go their extra burden, abandoning crystal droplets to the waiting earth.

If you want to hear God, listen to a thousand voices rejoicing. Listen to the lark, the crow, the loon.

Listen as the thunder grows distant and a perfect stillness embraces the earth.

If you want to hear God, listen.

Small Wonders

  Clothed in majesty and fierce might, He dwells in the unbounded expanse beyond mortal constraints of time and space. Inapproachable light, greater than the sum of every star which burns in the deepest heavens, blazes out from the core of His being. By His sheer will were those heavens formed; "Let there be…" and it came to pass. Every grand wonder that has ever met human eyes, and those never yet seen, are but dim, vaporous shadows… reflections of grander things above. There, in the realm of the spirituals, reality is truly real.
  "Oh, what is man, that You are mindful of him?" Wretched, puny man… so frail and fallen from the grand design… Why should He consider mere dust? And yet, He who measured out the seas in the palm of His hand crafted the atoms of which those waters are made. A limitless God in childlike delight chose the colors for each wildflower and dabbled the spots on

the ladybug. He paints the morning and evening skies and scatters the clouds above; a limitless God, enraptured by limitless love. Though He stands above all and His voice in majesty thunders, yet this limitless God of limitless love delights in small wonders.

The Knowing

Wisdom is bought
in quiet moments,
when self dissolves
and becomes absorbed
by a higher realm.

Solitude begets a knowing
unmatched by scholarly gain.
Hours invested
in focused repose
are never spent in vain.

Chains

   A love eternal, unsearchably vast… a passion divine, spilling itself with abandon upon tiny creatures who crawl around a pale blue-green ball, addicted to sorrow--- the shackles of grief and confusion, their dearest friends. The chains of shame, which tear the soul, keep their heads bowed low, embracing the dust and filth… spending their full measure of affection on that which enslaves and consumes.

   Finally, love can bear no more. He who is above all, who holds all of creation within His hand, spends the last desperate measure of devotion. The author of eternity steps down into time, enfolding Himself into the very form and appearance of fallen man. Radiance and power which would shame a billion suns hides itself behind a veil of flesh, invading the darkened land. Now face to face with the very object of His love, that veil is torn and light breaks free. Chains dissolve; darkness flees.

Echoes of Tomorrow

There's a new world coming. Beyond the flames of ignorance and greed, beyond the cries of despair and the schemes of hateful men, do you hear it? Can you hear the trumpet's voice and the song of Moses and of the Lamb? Do you hear the joyful shouts of the redeemed... echoes of tomorrow?

Can you hear the approaching hoof-beats, pulsing faster... faster... faster... like the heartbeat of a lovesick God, half mad with passion for His bride?

Can you sense; do you know the fire in His eyes...the fires of passion and rage, ready in an instant to pour out vengeance upon the destroyer of men's souls?

There's a new world coming, and the heavens will soon pass away at the voice of His command.

Introducing YWAM Faith Harvest Helpers:

"To know God and to make Him known..." This is the motto and the guiding principle of Youth With A Mission International. Within this framework, Faith Harvest Helpers plays a vital role in *sharing food* and *giving hope*. Processing and distributing food as well as medical supplies and other essentials to needy people at home and worldwide, Faith Harvest Helpers is a vital and growing ministry centered around the principles and aspirations of Matthew 25:35... "For I was hungry and you gave me something to eat, I was thirsty and you gave me something to drink." It is this heart of servant-evangelism in meeting the needs of a hungry world –both physical and spiritual- which defines YWAM Faith Harvest Helpers.

Beginnings...

For over 20 years, members of Faith Harvest Helpers have made the yearly trek to YWAM Gleanings in California to help glean and process food which is sent to hungry people around the globe. During one of these trips, a vision was born to do something with surplus food in the Pacific Northwest. In 2006, Faith Harvest Helpers incorporated as a 501c3 and began processing surplus salmon from Washington State hatcheries to share with those in need. In 2010, we grew to closely partner with a distribution center located in Yelm, Washington where fresh fruit, vegetables, bread, and dairy products could be distributed as well.

Growing...

Locally, approximately one million pounds of donated food is now processed and distributed by members and volunteers of Faith Harvest Helpers annually. This includes vegetables, bread, fruit, salmon, and dairy products. This is distributed by a small army of volunteers to benefit Pacific Northwest food banks and feeding programs.

Globally, we partner with a variety of other ministries to distribute non-perishable food, Christian literature, medical supplies, hygiene items, and other commodities with a message of hope.

Looking towards the future, we have purchased a 30 acre farm property in the rural outskirts of Olympia, Washington and are busy converting it into a new and expanded ministry center. This will allow us to consolidate all ministry operations into one location, thus maximizing efficiency and good stewardship of resources. It will also vastly expand the opportunities for ministry and growth.

Construction plans include warehouses, dorms, kitchens, a chapel, administrative offices, a training and discipleship facility, and large greenhouses. As plans unfold, we will be growing much of our own food to supplement donated items, utilizing state- of-the-art hydroponic technology.

We will also develop a commercial cannery for fish and other commodities and continue in the role of "making disciples" through YWAM's Discipleship Training School and other educational opportunities.

Jump on board!

For information on how to volunteer, donate, or join an outreach, please contact paul@faithharvesthelpers.org.

You are also invited to visit our website: www.ywamfhhwa.org.

Find out more about the global ministry of Youth With A Mission at www.ywam.org.

Gifts or requests for additional information may also be sent to:

YWAM Faith Harvest Helpers, 12643 Case Road SW, Olympia, WA 98512

Additional titles by Michael M. Middleton:

Modern Musings
The Great Deep, revised edition
Whispers of the Divine
Shadows and Substance
Sketches and Reflections
Waves of Glory
Daily Grace, volume one
Daily Grace, volume two
Daily Grace, volume three
Daily Grace, volume four
Get Real, the pitfall of a cultural Christianity
On Guard, ministering Christ in a messed up world
Castles in the Sky and other tales

All titles available at
www.amazon.com/author/mmm

...And By Sharon Middleton:

On Winds of Change

A large variety of inspirational gift items incorporating the author's writing, photography, and other art work may be found at: www.Zazzle.com/Mgifts.

Made in the USA
Columbia, SC
02 December 2017